THE START OF SOMETHING

BIG

(or how to find an idea to make money)

by

Maureen Larter

CHAPTER ONE

Making money has never been easy. There are many books out in the world telling you HOW to market your business, how to use social media to pack a punch, how to get websites dragging in the clients, BUT... what if you have no business or business idea? Where do you start, how do you find something that YOU can do to make an income, small or otherwise?

We often have to be in the right spot at the right time. But one thing that helps is having "the idea" in the first place. This booklet will help you in your search for "THE IDEA" and how you can put it into practice.

Once you have that idea there are some requirements you must cultivate within yourself if you wish to make it into a successful money-making venture.

1. The first is ORGANIZATION
2. Another is PERSERVERANCE and
3. You will need to WORK HARD

Nothing that is worth doing will simply fall into your lap - these three attributes are necessary.

I am presuming that at the moment you are NOT making money. Perhaps you are unemployed or on a pension and that is why you have decided to invest in this booklet. If you are already working, but are not satisfied with your lot and want to do something about it, then the tips and techniques in this booklet will still be relevant.

However, at this time I will consider that you are not working and therefore not getting paid. If you volunteer with any charity, by definition, that still means that you receive no payment for your time.

Perhaps your day is broken down into something like this - 8 hours of sleep, 3 hours eating and preparing to eat, 4 hours watching TV or playing games, or being distracted on Facebook, 2 hours not doing very much at all, 3 hours visiting/playing or procrastinating or... maybe that's not quite your routine - but you get the picture.

My philosophy is easy. From the moment you are born to the moment you die, you exist in time. Therefore, if you wish to make the most of this life, you must live every minute of every day whether you get paid for the privilege or not. Time is, therefore, not really worth anything. However, depending on your activities, you can make it worth whatever your heart desires.

If you find an "idea" to make some money then your time becomes worth something. Even if it is only $2 an hour, that's $48 a day or $336 a week for every hour of your existence. So that's more money than you would have made if you had stayed at home watched TV, eaten, sleep, played games on your mobile (cell phone) or communicated with friends on Facebook.

Now I'm not advocating that you work 24 hours a day, 7 days a week, but my point is that ANYTHING you make is better than nothing! So even if you work only 5 hours a week, you would still have $10 you didn't have before. Obviously it would be better if you worked more, or had a better hourly rate.

In the economic climate in which we live, not only is it more difficult to live comfortably, but it is not easy to get other people to part with their money. Remember, other people struggle to make ends meet as well.

So, when you start out with your business, be organized, practical, sensible and determined - BUT DON"T BE GREEDY!

Think about what YOU would spend, or are able to spend.

If you are starting out you are probably conscious of your budget, so consider that others are in the same boat. Most people are looking for a service or product at a reasonable cost.

Any purchased product should be of good quality and not fall apart at the first sign of stress.

Any service that is bought, should be delivered by a reliable, well qualified person and also be done well.

It is better to do a job well, or sell a product you have faith in, than receive the bad publicity from an unhappy customer. Word of mouth is your best friend if you are reliable, or your product is excellent; it can be your worst enemy if you take short cuts in both product or service.

When I first started out in a self-employed capacity, I worked on a simple principle. If my product cost $5 to make, then I charged $10 for that item. That then covered the cost of $5 for another product, with $5 for the cost of the product in the first place. It didn't really matter how long it took me to make or buy product, as I would have still had to exist (pass the time, living my life).

In this day of Internet and ebooks, this booklet may have taken me months to write, but once it is ready, it can be downloaded with a push of a button, with no more input from me. I can forego the 'plan' of product buying I used to start out with. If I can get 1,000 people to download it, my profit is assured, even at only $.99c a download.

However that is not the case with other types of products or services you might offer.

The rule of thumb as stated above for products pricings is OK, but how do you price a service that is based solely on time and your own knowledge?

Services can be tricky. It all depends on what you are qualified to do. Is it legal for you to put yourself forward as a plumber, merely because you have fixed the tap washers in your home?

I don't think so.

If your desire is to make your business around being a plumber - then make sure you get some qualifications first.

Having acquired your knowledge and with it the ability to do your job correctly, within the guidelines of the law, you now have to work out your pricing.

What would you be prepared to pay for your services? Are there any other plumbers/service people in your chosen field in your area? If so, what are they charging? Is there a niche that you can cover without any competition?

There are many things to think about before you take the plunge and begin. However, don't let that put you off. Consider the fact that there are a lot of cleaners out in the world, but there is always room for one more!

Now, let's presume you have three good competitors in your field. How much do they charge. As you are just starting out, it might be wise to price yourself just over the lowest price, or you might want to charge a little lower still. This will help you get a foot in the door and create a client base so that you can build your reputation. (Be careful you don't go too cheap - otherwise some people will presume your work is shoddy! - you can always increase your charges, but it is unwise, and difficult, to decrease!). Don't under-rate yourself, but, on the other hand, don't charge beyond what people in your area are able to pay.

If you used to live in the city and are now starting a business in the country, don't presume that you can get the same sort of rates at your new address. Be very conscious of the going rate in your neighbourhood, whether it be in the middle of a city, large country town, small village, or rural expanse!

Get as much knowledge about your chosen product or service as you can..

Obtain any qualifications you may need.

Check the need for your business.

Do your research.

CHAPTER TWO

After you have your 'idea, you must organize yourself so that you work on your business for at least an hour a day, six days a week (we always need one day off - the old saying about all work and no play has validity!).

Pick a time that is normally quiet and unproductive and make it your hour. No distractions! Fit it in to your routine of living, whether you feel like it or not (that's called discipline!). That way you will move forward in your business and achieve progress for six hours every week. Don't cheat by doing all six hours in one day and then sit back smugly for the rest of the week.

When you first begin you will be enthusiastic, and one hour will suddenly become, three or four without any difficulty and you will wonder where the time went.

Don't be fooled.

You should still come back the next day and do your hour. It is far better to bite off little chunks of work and be consistent with it. Setting a good habit is crucial, because there will come a time where the whole business will pall. Perhaps things aren't going as well as you thought, or the process becomes bogged down in boring paperwork or foot work. This is when your persistence and organization will be an absolute necessary part of moving onwards and upwards.

The whole process of making a decent living should come gradually. Nobody wants to start a flood of work which will over power you and end up sending you into a downward spiral of unreliability or stress resulting in illness thereby causing even more problems.

Pace yourself - learn to tell your customers/clients the truth and keep them on side if you are finding your time is being sabotaged and you are not getting everything done (maybe this is the time you will have to look for help from an employee).

If you happen to be on unemployment benefits, or some type of pension, you are permitted to earn a certain amount each week before you start to lose this financial lifeline.

There are schemes the government in Australia has put into place to encourage people wishing to start a business (the New Enterprise Incentive Scheme

(N.E.I.S.) comes to mind) and it doesn't hurt to find out what is available in your country before you start any venture. It is always changing.

Be careful. If you tell the authorities you are going to be self-employed, your benefit may be withdrawn or reduced and that will make it difficult to survive.

It is far better for your well-being and general health (and those around you that may depend on you) if you know you can gradually increase your income, and in the process, wean yourself off any benefit or pension until you no longer come under the Government's jurisdiction. This can be done quite legally and above board, so don't be frightened to enquire BEFORE you start. You should be aware that if you leave informing Centrelink (in Australia) or other agencies until after you start earning an independent income, you may have to pay back past benefits.

My suggestion, once you have worked out your commitments, is to make an appointment with your Government services and take in a profit and loss statement, if required, and be as honest as you can to cover the worry of being 'dobbed' in by someone with nothing better to do with their time.

If you have any problems with this approach, I would be pleased to hear from you. If the government penalizes you when you are obviously trying to improve your lot in life, it seems to me we need to use our strength of numbers to put pressure on the government to change their attitude so that they can encourage people to be honest and open (I don't think this is the position at this time!!).

Having been in the position of being on benefits myself, I found it was difficult to keep my self-esteem high, and not let my confidence and initiative be depleted. It can be difficult to stay motivated, particularly if everyone around you is negative and putting obstacles in your path.

Don't give up! You are worth more than that.

If you are not on any government payment, but are working for a company, it is your right to do something out of working hours, whether it be a hobby, a sport, or a new business - although it would be wise to check your employment contract as some activities could be seen as a conflict of interest.

Make sure you keep a written tally of all your expenses as well as income. If you are no accountant, then keep it simple. Buy a plain, lined exercise book. Make a list of expenses in the front, and a list of income in the back. This gives you an idea of your profit or loss, and shows you are serious about your business. You cannot be taxed or penalized for a loss, as long as progress can be seen in your endeavor.

Another avenue to pursue would be the registration of a business name and obtaining an ABN (Australian Business Number if you live in Australia) In Australia, an ABN is free, but there is a small charge for a business name, which can be acquired online through ASIC - the Australian Securities and Investments Commission. Check for similar Government bodies in your country. Again, be sure you are making the business a serious venture and realize that it may then no longer be regarded as a hobby for taxation purposes. If that is what you want, or is the legal way to go if you are making enough money, then so be it. A hobby is one way of beginning a business without being penalized.

By the way, it is possible to have a business without registering the name - as long as you are using your name in the title. (e.g. 'Fred Smith's Horse-Shoeing' or 'Kevin and Mary Brown's House-cleaning Service').

Just a word of warning before we proceed further - when you start getting money/income from your new business, it is very easy to fritter it away in general living, particularly if you have been on a very tight budget.

DO NOT put the money in your purse.

KEEP THE BUSINESS MONEY COMPLETELY SEPARATE.

This money must be put back into the business - the expenses may be high when you start, and this can be the downfall of your business. There is the cost of advertising, product or materials to make your product, equipment that you use for your work, petrol for travelling etc.

If you wish to reward yourself for your labour, take only a small percentage, and only after all expenses have been deducted and the next job is already covered. (From every $10 you bring in, only 50c may be available to you to spend!)

So far I have given you advice on attitude, organization and money management for your business.

So ... how do we get that idea?

How do we find something that will make us a living? What are we going to do as our business?

CHAPTER THREE

Right! Let's find that idea. Your idea. The idea that fits you and your abilities. The idea that will create a viable business.

The first secret is to look at yourself and the things you do and love to do. A hobby is a good place to start.

A hobby that you already do has some obvious advantages.

Firstly, you probably have a lot of the equipment at your fingertips anyway, and

Secondly, you enjoy your hobby, otherwise you wouldn't be doing it.

Both of these reasons are important when you try to formulate a money-making venture. When you work for someone else, the job can be boring, uninteresting and even degrading, but... you can walk away at the end of the working day and be your own person, forgetting the job for a while.

When you decide to work for yourself it isn't nearly so easy to 'turn off'. Therefore, enjoying your line of work is so much better. As with everything that becomes a necessary day in day out activity, it can become frustrating and depressing at times. If you enjoy what you are doing, when the going gets tough, you can pull on that reserve of enthusiasm and enjoyment you felt at the beginning and that will get you through.

Don't kid yourself - it happens to everyone. When things are at rock bottom everyone goes through thinking 'Why am I doing this?' and wants to give up.

DON'T.

As long as you keep your financial purse strings under control, there is no reason to give up. Be aware however, that it is extremely easy to try and expand too quickly and thereby get yourself into hot water both with your finances and stress levels, let alone finding yourself time poor, tired and not able to find the strength and enthusiasm to continue.

My advice is to only do what you can afford to do. Only take on what you can cope with. If you need money to buy materials for either product or service, don't be afraid to ask your customers/clients for a deposit.

People do understand, and if they don't, maybe you didn't need their order in the first place.

So where is the idea? What do you do now?

Let's look at some scenarios, and then try to put yourself in place of the people I have given as examples.

CASE ONE.

Jane is sitting at her spinning wheel enjoying her hobby of spinning wool to make articles for her family and friends. How can she turn this into a viable business to make a little (or a lot) of income?

Here are some ideas.

a) Jane can teach others how to spin.

b) Jane can sell the garments she makes from the spun wool, particularly the unique dressing-gown she has designed and loves to make.

c) Jane can't find enough wool to continue with her hobby, so she can start looking for unusual fleeces and supply others with fleeces, too.

d)Jane became so interested in wool, she decided to take a course in wool-classing and can then become a 'Travelling Classer' for sheep stations around Australia. This combined her love of wool with her love of travel.

e) Jane decides to breed up a pair of sheep so she can use their fleeces. She can then start a 'fleece' farm and supply others with wool (it is advantageous to have property for this)

f) Jane has got an acreage. At present she has no animals of her own, so she agists the space for other people's animals. (This means people pay her a 'rent' for each head of cattle/sheep or horses that graze on her property).

g) One of the parts of her spinning wheel is always breaking and it is difficult to find replacements. Jane works out a different product that does the same job, makes it and then supplies others with the part.

h) After some experimenting, Jane works out how to extract the lanolin from her wool and makes up hand cream and sells it.

i) The part of spinning and weaving that fascinates Jane is natural dying of the wool after it is spun. She decides to write a 'how to' booklet to help others do the same.

j) Some of the dyes she has made are unique, so she bottles them and sells them.

k) Jane loves to knit her own hand spun wool into beautiful garments. She sells them to local and interstate boutiques and, with the help of the internet, expands out into the world.

l) Jane writes out her patterns and sells the pattern books.

m) Jane starts a spinners club, charges a small memberships fee, then a small fee for swapping fleeces and spinning wheels, using the club and group and an e-store on Facebook to combine all her business ideas.

n) Jane writes a 'how to' book on how to spin and then use the spun wool.

o) Her grandchildren adore the fluffy slippers Jane makes from the wool, so she makes more and sells them at markets as a specialized line (with her other garments and books).

p) The carded wool bits that are left over make terrific stuffing for soft toys. She bags it and sells it to craft shops.

q) She makes and designs soft toys, stuffs them with her wool cardings, sells them and writes a pattern book as well.

r) Jane decides to try spinning 'exotic' wools as a greater challenge. Mohair, rabbit, dog and alpaca open up a completely new range of business ideas.

As you can see, from one activity there are a multitude of ideas which can become businesses - as small or as large as your energy can make them. Several of these ideas are already in practice by friends of mine, so they are proven and working well. Remember, your individual stamp gives you the edge in any business you undertake.

Let's try another interest.

Can we change a seemingly normal male hobby into a business?

CASE TWO

Damian loves to watch footy on T.V. and if he had the money, he would go to all the games he could. His wife is always cranky because he spends too much time in front of the TV and does nothing else with his mates but discuss football. This seems to be a hard hobby to get a business out of.

Let's see what comes to mind (perhaps you can think of more).

a) Damian takes a course and gets a paid job being a coach/umpire for the youngsters in his area.

b) Damian organizes three of his friends' wives (and his own - if she wants to become involved) who love knitting, to make football scarves, socks and beanies and sells them at the local markets. Small knitted mascots for key-rings or other uses might be a novel idea too. He adds all sorts of football memorabilia to his stall as well. He can learn to knit and while he sits at the markets he can be knitting scarves - it will be an attraction for his potential customers.

c) Damian starts a newsletter about his local team and sells it at a small cost to people at the local games when his team is playing. This product is also added to the stall mentioned above.

d) Damian writes a 'how to' book for beginners about the game, with all the rules and how to understand them, as well as exercises and tips to help play the game.

e) Damian designs and sells trophies which he can sell to the different football clubs in his area - or in fact, further afield. This can become a viable online business.

f) Damian organizes 'footy' parties for groups of people who are as mad about the game as he is.

g) Damian works out charts of all the scores of all the games and can run a betting ring to see who wins - like Melbourne Cup sweeps. This may mean he will have to register a betting business - check the legal requirements of this idea!

Needless to say, being someone who detests the game of football, I can't think of as many suggestions - but I could still come up with several ideas.

Can you think of any other ideas that could generate an income from this hobby?

If you can, please let me know when you set up your business.

NOTES

CASE THREE.

Here are some ideas for a business where both partners have a common interest. In this case, Jim and Mary love gardening. They have a beautiful garden, but now it only needs maintenance and they would like to expand their horizons. What can they do?

a) They start a home-garden maintenance business and help others to get their gardens under control. This could expand into a landscaping consultancy.

b) Mary has lots of plants she can propagate from cuttings. They set up a hot-house and supply new plants.

c) After collecting seeds from their plants, seedlings are organized into punnets and sold at the local market. A wholesale business to nurseries can be an addition as well.

d) Their vegetable patch is really prolific. They supply vegetables to their local greengrocer.

e) Flowers are more their interest. They supply florists with their beautiful blooms.

f) Jim tends the vegetable garden, and Mary loves cooking, so they manufacture jams, pickles and preserves and sell the products. Please note any council conditions in this last idea. There is the possibility that you may need a 'commercial' kitchen. If this is the case, before going to that expense, it might be worth it to rent a commercial kitchen until the budget can stand the expense.

g) Jim constructs several compost bins and they make compost, bag it up and sell it.

h) By having a herb garden, Mary and Jim pick and dry herbs, make fragrant sachets and similar products and sell them.

i) Jim and Mary pot up several lush indoor plants and start a plant hire enterprise for offices and other businesses. This attracts a small weekly fee for maintenance of these plants.

j) Mary suggest a modification to a handy weeding tool and Jim makes a prototype. It is a success, so they manufacture and sell them.

k) They collect seeds from the non-hybrid plants and package them for sale.

l) They collaborate and write booklets on how to plan a garden, what and when to plant and what to make from the produce out of the back-yard garden. This can then be self-published and marketed through the Internet.

m) Hydroponics interests them but they find it hard to get supplies of the necessary components, so they find a supplier, then start a business in their area, selling those products.

n) Jim is really good at pruning and espalier work, so he writes a booklet on that aspect of his garden. Mary loves photography and takes all the photos for his book. He starts teaching his knowledge as well.

o) They both take a course in bonsai and sell their efforts, go on to teach others and write a 'how-to' book about it.

p) They decide to travel around Australia, visiting open gardens. They write a guide for all the gardens they see.

As you can see, it is easy to start a money-making venture. The most important pre-requisite is to start with something you know and love, whether it be gardening, knitting, art, reading, cooking or anything else at all.

CHAPTER FOUR

As a self-published author, one of my options would be to offer my services to others who wish to publish a book. I can have a business as a publisher, or an agent, or both!

If you think you have no particular interest or talent, then ask around your friends and find out if there is anything they hate doing and would be willing to pay someone else to do for them. There are all sorts of ideas:-

a) Cleaning ovens

b) Cleaning concrete driveways

c) Weeding the garden

d) Mowing lawns

e) Cleaning windows

I'm sure you can think of more. I have made a list of everything I could think of that may be able to create an income for you. Think about any of these which might appeal to you.

- Affiliate selling through the Internet
- Agent for other professionals
- Any product you feel is unusual or individual to you.
- Art work
- Babysitting
- Blacksmithing and Ironmongery
- Book binding service for any booklets written (I can offer this service)
- Buckle supplies
- Buy a business that is already up and running (if you have the money)
- Café owner
- Cake making and/or decorating
- Candle making
- Chalkboard signs
- Chef
- Children's clothes
- Computer graphics/web design/word processing services
- Consultant in any field you are highly qualified in
- Doll making

- Dressmaking and repairs
- EBook publishing
- Editing of other people's books
- Educational toys
- Findings for craft - leather goods/jewelry etc
- Finger nail painting
- Florist supplies and flowers
- Garden and lawn maintenance
- Garden ornaments/pots manufacture
- Handyman service
- Hat making (Akubra had to start somewhere!)
- Herbal bouquets and infusions
- Herbal cosmetics and creams
- House cleaning - both inside or outside
- 'How-to' books on ANY subject (just like this booklet you are reading)
- Indoor plant maintenance
- Invitation design and printing
- Ironing
- Jam/pickle/chutney/preserve etc making
- Jewelry making
- Joke books
- Knife making
- Leather craft
- Lingerie making
- Manicuring
- Material and sewing supplies
- Mobile coffee and tea/lunch van
- Music teaching (piano/violin/guitar/drums etc)
- Notepad/envelope/greeting card making
- Office cleaning
- Old-fashioned toys (e.g. rag books)
- Outdoor furniture manufacture
- Party organization
- Pastry and fancy cake making
- Pattern books (anything from knitting to blacksmithing)
- Pedicure
- Pet grooming

- Pet sitting
- Plant rental
- Plant sitting
- Pottery (but be different - there is a lot around)
- Products from recycled items
- Puzzle and activity books
- Recipe books
- Seedling starter business
- Silversmithing
- Small appliance repair
- Small carpentry repair
- Soap making
- Soft toys
- Swimwear and gym wear
- Teaching
- Wedding/portrait photography
- Window cleaning

etc etc - add your own here.

If you need to learn how to start a business, there are plenty of places which offer courses.

If you like to read, the library and Google will be able to help with a lot of information. This is important if your budget doesn't stretch to the cost of some of the courses that are available.

I'm sure I haven't thought of everything, so feel free to think up some other ideas.

CHAPTER FIVE

So - let's do a quick review of the suggestions in this booklet.

Pick something you like are good at doing or want to try.

For example - cooking, fishing, woodwork, country music, gardening, knitting, photography, playing the piano, drawing, reading, eating, in fact anything you can imagine. Everybody likes something. Then you can:-

- Make products associated with your likes (specialize in something unusual if you can).
- Teach it to someone else.
- Write a booklet about it.
- Find a product that is allied to it that is difficult to find.
- Retail any and all products or service.
- Start clubs or a group on Facebook (get a data-base through your blog or website) of like-minded people who may be interested to become your clients/customers.
- Look at what is already in the market place - see if you can do it better/cheaper.
- Is there a 'hole' in the market place of a product you would like. Source it and sell it.
- Find a service you would like to have available and do it yourself.

All these suggestions should help you on your path to 'your idea'.

It is not easy to come up with something that has not been done before. It can be done. If you have an inventive mind, there are always products that can be improved or we would have never progressed. Even in this age of technology, liquid paper has been discovered, and even a new type of bee hive. If you have something commonplace - like winter pyjamas for instance - if you can produce it well then it is a viable product. Everyone is an individual and brings something new to any product or service.

You must also remember that not everyone will like your idea, but not everyone will hate it either. There are millions of people in Australia, let alone the whole world (I think it was 7.2 billion at last guesstimate) and each person is different and has their own particular likes and dislikes, so you have a market out there.

Working on small percentages and statistics - if you do it right, you WILL make money.

Before you sell/make or manufacture anything, make sure that you have followed all the government guidelines and regulations in your part of the world.

There is no excuse doing anything 'on the sly'. It will only be your downfall if you are caught.

Before you begin save up enough money for equipment and anything else you need while you are reading and learning as much as possible about your desired business idea.

CHAPTER SIX

Of course, once you have your idea, you then have to implement it and keep it going. That is where marketing comes in.

Today, with such a lot of social media at your fingertips, it can be quite daunting.

There are many people out there willing to take your money to give you advice on Marketing.

Be aware.

Social Media can cost quite a lot of money if you want to advertise. Facebook, Twitter and similar type sites are clamping down on the out and out selling procedures and the reach of your comments aren't nearly so wide-spread as they once were. However, with careful and clever planning, these can be free and used to your advantage. Again, be conscious that they can also take up a lot of your time and effort. You can still find 'experts' willing to sell you books, courses and webinars on how to do just that.

Just how do you get your customers? They won't just fall at your feet and offer you their money. To gain customers, you have to put in work and effort, just make sure you don't neglect your product/service along the way.

Here are a few ideas that will help.

As I am showing you the simplest and cheapest way to get started, my first recommendation is to advertise in your local paper. Unfortunately, in this day and age, newspapers are becoming less and less used so find the 'local' website and advertise there.

I've already mentioned 'word-of-mouth' advertising. When you start out, tell all your friends and acquaintances what you do. Again, be mindful that some people will only give you negative feedback - don't take any notice. Keep telling everyone you meet.

Once you get a job remember this - word-of-mouth is your best friend - if you do a good job or have a wonderful product. But it can also be your worst enemy. They say that a satisfied customer will tell a couple of friends (who may tell a couple of friends) but an unhappy customer will tell everyone!

As you go along, try as many different ways of advertising that you can think of. Make sure you always have the money to pay for whatever you do.

Some will work - some won't.

Budget a certain amount of money per month and get started.

You can put a classified advert in your local paper for a reasonable amount - and try it for 1 month, 3 months, 6 months or a year - whatever you can afford. Try bulletin boards at your local shopping mall, make flyers and place them in retail outlets, or walk around and do a letterbox drop in your immediate area.

If it doesn't work at first, have a break, but don't give up.

Try again and again if necessary.

Some products and services will find markets as an ideal platform for you. You will need equipment and be prepared to pack and unpack your vehicle, and work on weekends as well as get up in the dark to beat your venue in plenty of time to set-up.

Whatever you can think of, and what works for you is worth a try.

One of the problems you will encounter is that once you are 'in business' everyone suddenly thinks you are rich and you will be pestered for donations from representatives of all types of charities as well as advertisers. Pick a charity which you would like to support and say no to all the others. Only advertise when and where you can afford to. No use advertising 'chickens for sale' in a crossword puzzle edition of a magazine! Far better to pick an agricultural or self-sufficiency type magazine or website.

Another couple of things that come to mind are HOW you present yourself, your product or your service. You must treat this in a business-like manner and make sure you sound confident, but not pushy. Dress in smart and clean clothes that fit your type of business. No-one expects a plumber to wear a suit or an accountant to wear a navy singlet (vest), shorts and thongs (flip flops)!

One of the more important items which help businesses are business cards. These present a professional impression and can be given out to everyone. It is much easier to read than remember from a chance encounter, and it can be used in the future when suddenly the customer may want your product or service.

Keep your business card simple and clear.

Make sure you have all the necessary information on it, without it being cluttered. You should have your business name (if you have one), your name, your telephone number, website address, email address if you wish and, of course what you do or are offering.

Make sure the colors complement each other and everything is easy to read. Keep it as simple as you can.

The best way to get business cards (it is expensive to get them done by a local printer) is online. Vistaprint.com is one of the best sites. However, don't take my word for it - shop around for the best price.

Not competent on a computer? Get a friend to help. Better still take a course and learn how and what to do yourself - computers are not going to go away, and you need to know how to do anything you want using current technology. That means you should keep up to date at all times.

If you are selling a service, consider organizing a basic uniform, with your name and company name printed on the front of a shirt or its pocket. And always have some business cards in that pocket to hand out!

Do you sell a product? Does it need packaging? Packaging is extremely important. I like to think seriously about what exactly packaging should be. Try to consider recycling, or at least make your packaging able to be used again later. Waste is such a huge problem now, so if you can keep that to a minimum you are helping the environment. You must also take into account that your product should look professional (and clean). Cheap goods use cheap packaging, and this will not help your sales.

CHAPTER SEVEN

Let's look at the points once again.

1) Find an idea to make money from your own hobbies, talents and likes.

2) Buy an exercise book and record all monies spent and received.

3) Keep it as a hobby to begin with until you iron out all the problems.

4) Name your business with your own name or, if you wish, register a special name (this will cost money).

5) Tell everyone about your business.

6) Find the cheapest advertising in the classifieds of your local paper - or use the Internet and local groups or websites.

7) Get some nice, clear and colorful business cards.

8) Package your goods carefully and use eye-catching and consistent labels.

9) Don't overspend - save the money up before you do each step. If you need a lot of money, consider Internet 'crowd-funding' sites.

10) Don't be greedy - keep your rates affordable for the average struggling family.

11) Don't give up.

12) Be organized at all times.

13) Keep your business money completely separate from normal living expenses.

14) Always do your job or make your product to the best of your ability.

15) Always be polite to your customers - word of mouth will be your best friend. Handle any complaints with fairness and cheerfulness.

16) Be reliable.

17) Be on time for all jobs and appointments.

18) Don't argue with your customers!

19) Present yourself professionally

20) Make sure you are up to date with all the latest technology. Learn anything you need to know.

21) Keep everything legal and above board.

CHAPTER EIGHT

Now it's your turn -:

If you think you have no particular interest or talent, then what do you do?

Ask around your friends and find out if there is anything they hate doing and would be willing to pay someone else to do - like cleaning ovens, concrete driveways or windows!

See if there is anything in your town that is not catered for and has to be obtained in another town - then, if you have the ability to do it, fill the gap.

These days many people buy online - consider setting up your business on the 'net, or become an affiliate for another company.

If you need inspiration or more information, Google it, or go to the local library and read everything you can to help you in your undertaking.

Write down your hobbies, likes or talents now:

a)

b)

c)

d)

e)

f)

g)

h)

i)

j)

Write down some ideas (however silly you think they might be) that come from the list above:-

a)

b)

c)

d)

e)

f)

g)

h)

i)

j)

k)

l)

m)

n)

o)

p)

q)

r)

s)

t)

u)

v)

Write down your expected immediate needs and expenses:-

a)

b)

c)

d)

e)

f)

g)

h)

Think about the following:-

Do you need extra training?

Do you need licenses?

Do you need to be registered?

Are there any Health regulations?

Are there any laws you must follow?

How much will these things cost?

How will you price your time/product?

What would be a sensible starting capital?

Any other notes that you must consider:-

NOTES:-

And last but not least

GOOD LUCK.

Maureen Larter lives on the Mid North Coast of Australia, on a beautiful 15 acres. After working as a teacher at secondary school level, she decided to be independent of employers, and became self-employed. Now that she has retired, she turned her hand to writing. Her output has included garden guides, children's picture and chapter books and, just recently, an adult contemporary novel.

This little booklet is designed to help others who are struggling in an occupation they don't particularly like, or are dreaming of creating a better life for themselves.

Should you decided to look at my other titles, please feel free to go to:-

viewAuthor.at/MaureenLarter   or

readeatdream.net

If you would like to contact me I would appreciate any useful comments. My email is:

maureenlarter@gmail.com.

I intend to start a newsletter soon - if you have any ideas that you would like me to discuss, feel free to let me know.

If you decide to subscribe to that in the future, I will be sending out a free package as a thank you.

www.ingramcontent.com/pod-product-compliance
Lightning Source LLC
Chambersburg PA
CBHW060325220326
41598CB00027B/4427